No Rain, No Gain

Growing Through Life's Storms

Susan Lenzkes

Discovery House
PUBLISHERS

BOX 3566 · GRAND RAPIDS, MI 49501

*PUBLISHING BOOKS THAT FEED
THE SOUL WITH THE WORD OF GOD.*

Unless otherwise indicated, Scripture is taken from the Holy Bible: New International Version (North American Edition). Copyright © 1973, 1978, 1984 by the International Bible Society. Used by permission of Zondervan Bible Publishers.

Library of Congress Cataloging-in-Publication Data

Lenzkes, Susan L.
    No rain, no gain : growing through life's storms / Susan Lenzkes.
      p.   cm.
    ISBN 0-929239-93-8
    1. Consolation--Prayer-books and devotions--English.
  2. Spiritual formation.   3. Meditations.   I. Title.
  BV4909.L45   1995
  242'.4--dc20   94-48655
                                     CIP

Discovery House Publishers is affiliated with RBC Ministries, Grand Rapids, Michigan.

Discovery House books are distributed to the trade by Barbour Publishing, Inc., Uhrichsville, Ohio 44683.

Printed in the United States of America

04 05 06 07 08 / CHG / 7 6 5 4 3

To my dear sister and friend
Carol Wilda Fast
who knows all about persevering through precipitation.
I admire you greatly.

To all my brothers and sisters in Christ
from around the corner
and around the world
who have prayed, encouraged, and helped me
(as I struggled to write this final book of a series),
my husband, Herb (as he has battled cancer),
and our entire rain-drenched little family—
I want you to know that
this book (and its author) would not be in one piece today
were it not for your sustaining love and faithful prayers.
I'm asking our Lord to reward you as only He can.

Special thanks to
all the dear ones at Discovery House Publishers
(Bob DeVries and Carol Holquist—how wonderful you are!),
my editor, Julie Ackerman Link
(who waited patiently as I searched
for blessings in storm clouds),
and to the dear people of
Vista Grande Church
and Kaiser hospice
who are walking with us through
the valley of the shadow of death.
God bless you.

Introduction

I *didn't want to* write this book about rainstorms. The fact that you are now holding it in your hands is testimony to the gracious and faithful patience of both God and my publisher. Not that I didn't want to finish my fourth and final book in this series, I just dreaded having to deal with its difficult subject matter. Storms are bad enough without having to think about *growing* through them.

Trouble and trials have rained down in torrents this past year, eroding the familiar landscape of my life. The cold winds of fear and uncertainty have blown across our little family. Dark clouds of disease and death still hang low.

There have been times of sunshine and gentle sprinkles, but we have lived through enough squalls to last me for a while.

"Survival is good," I would say, reassuring myself, and then add, "Lord, if You *are* bringing growth through all of this, I'm grateful. But could you please tell me about it later when I am strong enough to cope with one more thing?"

When I could no longer delay dealing with "one more thing," I began delving into the Bible, and my heartaches, questions, and concerns met a concentrated dose of the truth of God.

Now I'm feeling rather foolish. And very excited. The fresh understandings and the glorious reminders that led to this book have been absolutely thrilling and exhilarating!

When did I start to believe that growing is just one more burden? It's true that trials, trouble, and struggles often precede, or even precipitate, growth. But I've already lived through a lot of the trials, so why let God's enemy rob me of the treasures!

God hid all of His vast riches in Christ, then asked me if I'd like to grow up in Him. I can't believe that I almost said, "I don't know, will it hurt? Let me think about it."

Yes! I want to grow up in Christ! Will you join me?

Treasures of Darkness

Ye fearful saints, fresh courage take, the clouds ye so much dread are big with mercy, and shall break in blessings on your head.
William Cowper

Within the depths of
His darkest clouds
God often seems to bury His
richest treasures—
    silver streaks of growth,
    sterling faith,
    precious, gleaming truths—
for His beloved children.
Has a dense cloud of
    doubt,

pain,
loss,
trouble,
frustration or
loneliness
settled over you, dear one?
Search out the treasures of darkness!
The riches of your Heavenly Father hide there—
with your name engraved in silver!

I will give you the treasures of darkness, riches stored in secret places, so that you may know that I am the LORD, the God of Israel who calls you by name.
—Isaiah 45:3

From now on I will tell you of new things, of hidden things unknown to you. They are created now and not long ago; you have not heard of them before today.   *—Isaiah 48:6–7*

I am the LORD, and there is no other; apart from me there is no God. I will strengthen you, though you have not acknowledged me, so that from the rising of the sun to the place of its setting men may know there is none besides me. I am the LORD, and there is no other. I form the light and create darkness, I bring prosperity and create disaster; I, the LORD, do all these things. . . . Turn to me and be saved, all you ends of the earth; for I am God, and there is no other. They will say of me, "In the LORD alone are righteousness and strength."

—*Isaiah 45:5–7, 22, 24*

Growing
Pains

Growing up isn't for sissies.
Mary Betcher

The difficult truth about truth is that it often requires us to change our perspectives, attitudes, and rules for living.

Change of any sort is seldom easy. And change that produces personal growth is never easy. Yet as we submit to the One Who never changes, He marvelously works in our lives.

I have a friend rich in the determination to grow. She is rich too in opportunities, for life dealt her a crushing load—one that offered only two choices: "fight" or "fold." She chose to fight, and invited me to join her.

As I walked with this friend through her struggles, I occasionally heard her wail, "Please, Lord, I don't want to grow anymore!"

But I knew she didn't really mean it. Other than unscheduled retreats beneath the covers of her bed for tears and talk with the Lord, she never stopped enlarging the house of her spirit.

I have watched her work at rebuilding the losses of her incredibly painful childhood and early adulthood. Continually she seeks to know and be known, love and be loved. Step by step she is living out the life-changing truth of God's redemptive love and power.

With joy I've seen her discover her worth and move into her potential in Christ. Over and over she has let go of her own pain to get on with the business of living and of serving others who are hurting.

It is only the discomfort of such continuous stretching that my friend bemoans. And I can't blame her, for growing pains are real.

Neither do I blame her for not fully appreciating her progress, for she doesn't have the beautiful view of the results that I have. I hope, though, that she can hear applause in my words and feel approval in my love.

Because growing up in Christ is surely the most difficult, courageous, exhilarating, and eternally important work any of us will ever do.

Speaking the truth in love, we will in all things grow up into him who is the Head, that is, Christ.
                                        —Ephesians 4:15

His divine power has given us everything we need for life and godliness through our knowledge of him who called us by his own glory and goodness. Through these he has given us his very great and precious promises, so that through them you may participate in the divine nature and escape the corruption in the world caused by evil desires.

But grow in the grace and knowledge of our Lord and Savior Jesus Christ. To him be glory both now and forever! Amen.   *—2 Peter 1:3–4; 3:18*

Grow Up to Be a Child

... and a little child will lead them, ...
Isaiah 11:6

Almighty God squeezed Himself tight
and became a little child.
Then He Who satisfies every living thing
fed His hunger at a woman's breast.
He Who never slumbers or sleeps
learned to sleep through the night.
He Who spoke all creation into being
learned to say, "please" and "thank you."
He Who made countless galaxies learned to count to ten.
And then He said,
Unless you, too, become like a little child,
you cannot enter the kingdom of heaven.

God's kingdom is confusing by this world's standards. To have life, we must give it away. To rule, we must serve. To grow up, we must become like a little child.

We came into this world as children—full of curiosity, wonder, creativity, honesty, openness, humility, confidence, simplicity, and trust. But blow by crushing blow this sinful world taught us to stop trusting and convinced us to start hiding ourselves away and to lie about our needs or use our creativity to meet them in wrong ways.

God came to us as a little child so that He could teach us to go back and become little children with an all-wise, all-powerful, constantly loving, and perfect Heavenly Father. Christ came to reclaim the children that sin stole away. It is safe to grow up in Him.

At that time the disciples came to Jesus and asked, "Who is the greatest in the kingdom of heaven?" He called a little child and had him stand among them. And he said: "I tell you the truth, unless you change and become like little children, you will never enter the kingdom of heaven. Therefore, whoever humbles himself like this child is the greatest in the kingdom of heaven. And whoever welcomes a little child like this in my name welcomes me."

—Matthew 18:1–5

To all who received him, to those who believed in his name, he gave the right to become children of God— children born not of natural descent, nor of human decision or a husband's will, but born of God. The Word became flesh and made his dwelling among us. We have seen his glory, the glory of the One and Only, who came from the Father, full of grace and truth.

—John 1:12–14

The Success
of Failure

We all stumble in many ways.
James 3:2

Some of life's clouds stay high above us and merely threaten. Some sprinkle or mist, and some pour torrents. Others seem to move right down to where we live, settle over us, and dim our view of who we are and what we can do.

One such cloud is the leaden fog bank of personal failure. It covers our souls like a damp blanket, depressing us and obscuring our judgment. Soon we are in danger of believing not simply that we have failed but that we are a *failure*. What a difference between the two!

To have *failed* is to have lived, tried, and been proven to be imperfect like everyone else. To have failed is to own more wisdom, understanding, and experience than do those who sit on life's sidelines playing it safe. To have failed is to claim a clearer knowledge of what not to do the next time. And to have failed is to have an opportunity to extend to ourselves the grace that God so freely extends to us.

We become a *failure* when we allow mistakes to take away our ability to learn, give, grow, and try again. We become a failure if we allow our transgressions to activate an internal voice of eternal self-blame and shame. We become a failure if we let the "shoulds" and the "if onlys" suck us into their mire. And we are a failure when we become content with failing.

The mire caused by our blunders, errors, and failings can become the quicksand that traps us in regret, or it can become the material we use to make building blocks of righteousness. God waits to give us another chance. His grace is well spent on fresh starts.

Cast your cares on the LORD and he will sustain you; he will never let the righteous fall.
—Psalm 55:22

If the LORD *delights in a man's way, he makes his steps firm; though he stumble, he will not fall, for the* LORD *upholds him with his hand.*

—Psalm 37:23–24

The LORD *upholds all those who fall and lifts up all who are bowed down.* —Psalm 145:14

To him who is able to keep you from falling and to present you before his glorious presence without fault and with great joy—to the only God our Savior be glory, majesty, power and authority, through Jesus Christ our Lord, before all ages, now and forevermore! Amen. —Jude 24–25

Feeling Insignificant

What awe,
what wonder,
for tiny man on
frail earth
to realize that
size
is no measure of
worth
in God's enormous eyes.

One of Satan's most effective ploys is to make us believe that we are small, insignificant, and worthless. And it's often a fairly easy job for him, for as we measure our small lives and sin-shriveled souls against the vast holiness of God, we realize that indeed we are insignificant!

But God's enemy deceives us by suggesting that this realistic assessment of ourselves, this appropriate, honest *humility* is actually *humiliation*. Such truth-twisting tactics keep us so low, so filled with shame that we can't begin to see ourselves as God has chosen to see us.

To view ourselves through our Creator's loving, tear-filled eyes, we need to climb Calvary's hill and look down from the cross of Christ—for that is where God declared that we are worth the life of His precious Son.

Such a holy, awesome sacrifice of love bestows inestimable worth to us, His beloved in Christ.

Ephesians 1:4–8 tells us that God "*chose us* in him before the creation of the world to be *holy and blameless* in his sight. In *love* he predestined us to be adopted as *sons* (and *daughters*) through Jesus Christ, in accordance with his *pleasure* and *will*—to the praise of his *glorious grace*, which he has *freely* given us in the One he loves. In him we have *redemption* through his blood, the *forgiveness of sins*, in accordance with the *riches* of God's grace that he *lavished* on us with all wisdom and understanding" (emphasis mine).

He also declares that He has not just sprinkled, but has "*poured out* His love into our hearts by the Holy Spirit whom he has given us" (Romans 5:5).

We are the temple of God. We have been bought at great price. And we are instructed to honor God with our bodies (1 Corinthians 6:19–20). How God honors us by His indwelling presence and love!

When I consider your heavens, the work of your fingers, the moon and the stars, which you have set in place, what is man that you are mindful of him, the son of man that you care for him? You made him a little lower than the heavenly beings and crowned him with glory and honor. You made him ruler over the works of your hands; you put everything under his feet . . . O LORD, our LORD, how majestic is your name in all the earth! —Psalm 8:3–9

"Do not be afraid, little flock, for your Father has been pleased to give you the kingdom."
—Luke 12:32

This Isn't Funny Anymore

The workshop of character is everyday life.
Maltbie D. Babcock

The four of us stood in the blazing sun amid sagebrush and road-side dust watching our car spew forth its heated opinion about our forcing it to climb mountain roads at its age. Any hope of making it to our niece's wedding on time seemed to be going up in smoke too.

My husband, Herb, and our officially ASE certified "World Class Auto Technician" son, Jeff, wore the look men wear when they know exactly what's happening but can't do a thing about it. My daughter-in-law, Margie, and I wore the look women wear when they see their husbands look like that but can't do a thing about it.

Herb was supposed to be videotaping the wedding.

Margie had agreed to coordinate the proceedings. I had promised to help my sister with last-minute details. And Jeff was to be one of the groomsmen; yet there he stood in shorts and sandals, poking around under the hood, making solemn pronouncements. "Looks like cooling system vapor lock. This car's going to need considerable time to cool off, a gallon or two of water, and some serious attention later."

We could have used a similar prescription. This wasn't just a bad day we were having; it was a "last straw" day. A sense of humor seemed way beyond my emotional reach, so I settled for a sense of balance.

"Just don't make things worse," I kept saying to myself. "Remain calm. If you can't say something good, try to focus on what needs to be done." So, as cars and trucks zoomed by, intent on reaching their destination, I stood by the car, its hood raised like a huge flag, and prayed for a solution.

Finally a knight in a shining white pick-up truck pulled over and offered assistance. He left with our name, location, and my sister's phone number, promising to call for help as soon as he reached town. At least she would know what had happened to us.

Several minutes later my brother and his family, on their way to the ceremony, rescued us in time to intercept the man my sister had dispatched after hearing of our plight.

At the wedding site we stuffed our unhappy bodies into suits and ties, dresses and pantyhose. We weren't the only ones feeling the heat, for the plea came, "Could you please take ice water to the thirsty bridal party?"

Thankful that I had arrived in time to help a little, I hurried to gather a pitcher of water and cups. Hands full, I kicked the screen door open only to have it slam back into the pitcher, sending a cascade of water down my face and dress. They drank what was left, I dried what I could.

In spite of delays, the wedding commenced. The bride was radiant—the groom nervous and tender—the minister (the bride's step-father) touching and genuine in his expressions of his love for them and for God. I passed tissues to my sister, my daughter, and my daughter-in-law. It's good to have experience in these matters.

After the reception, the guys headed down the

mountain. They watered the car and talked severely to it, but, unheeding, it stranded us again on the way home—this time in a desolate patch of freeway between someplace and someplace else. Our daughter and son-in-law were following us, however, so at least we had help available.

On the way to the gas station, the girls bubbled with annoying good cheer. This was a family adventure, they said. We were making a memory that we would surely talk and laugh about later.

They found a huge white enameled cooking pot in the trunk of our daughter's car and filled it with water for the radiator.

Herb rode in the passenger seat dangling the pot from his thumbs, solemnly explaining (as engineers tend to do) that he was demonstrating the highly effective "decoupling theory" to prevent sloshing and spills.

The girls were certain that this was fun.

I was certain that we didn't need this much fun.

I was tired. Exhausted, really. And nothing was very funny. The day had topped off a bad week, which had followed an even worse one, after an unbelievable month which pretty much matched the whole year.

When life's heavy storms come like that, one after another, you can find yourself reeling, staggering, going to your knees, adjusting, being knocked flat again, then struggling up in time to catch yet another blow.

The accumulated losses can become so overwhelming that it takes only the sprinkles of life's daily problems to tip your boat. Every distress feels like a disaster. Nothing looks like a simple aggravation that could, with a little perspective and humor, be turned into an adventure.

When I've lost my sense of humor, when I can no longer bend and flex with the day's stresses and distresses, I don't need to give my day or my attitude over to the Lord. I need to give myself to Him. If I hope to grow through life's sprinkles as well as its downpours, if I want to learn patience and perseverance and gain heavenly perspective, I need to hide in Him. Rest in Him. Find myself renewed in Him. He waits with healing in His wings.

Yet the LORD longs to be gracious to you; he rises to show you compassion. For the LORD is a God of justice. Blessed are all who wait for him!. . . How gra-

cious he will be when you cry for help! As soon as he hears, he will answer you. Although the LORD gives you the bread of adversity and the water of affliction, your teachers will be hidden no more, with your own eyes you will see them. Whether you turn to the right or to the left, your ears will hear a voice behind you, saying, "This is the way; walk in it." . . . He will also send you rain for the seed you sow in the ground, and the food that comes from the land will be rich and plentiful.
—Isaiah 30:18–21, 23

But for you who fear my name, the sun of righteousness will rise with healing in his wings. And you will go free, leaping with joy like calves let out to pasture.   —Malachi 4:2 TLB

Don't
Give Up

By perseverance the snails reached the ark.
Charles Hadden Spurgeon

We're *slow-brew* Christians in an instant world. Small wonder that we get discouraged with ourselves!

The world serves up instant food, instant entertainment, and instant credit. We're offered computers, fax machines, microwave ovens, automatic phone dialers, remote control televisions, Polaroid cameras, high-speed elevators, and quick copy machines. We reach for hot-line help, rapid-rise yeast, express mail, and automatic banking. We can travel in racy cars with high-octane fuel, supersonic jets, and even orbit the globe in space capsules.

Then comes the Christian, a foot soldier on a

straight and narrow path. "Follow Me," Jesus says. "Put one foot in front of the other in moment-to-moment obedience." (Nothing like an invitation to take a stroll on the freeway!)

Then Jesus tells us that if we follow Him, He'll make us "fishers of men" (Mark 1:17). What? Bait and wait? Mend and cast nets? Clean and preserve the catch? (An unattractive assignment with flash-frozen fish fillet in the local supermarket!)

Next we discover that our Lord commanded us to "bear fruit" (John 15:16). Fruit? Isn't that the stuff that starts with a seed and has a slow-growing tree in between?

Then come His instructions to "grow up into him who is the Head" (Ephesians 4:15). Growing up is the slowest thing that happens to a child . . . even slower than waiting for Christmas. And eagerness adds neither an inch to the stature nor a year to the calendar.

Growth isn't fast, yet it does yield high gains. Our Lord explains that "the testing of your faith develops perseverance. Perseverance must finish its work so that you may be mature and complete, not lacking anything" (James 1:3–4).

Still, it might help our patience and perseverance to realize that while there are no instant formulas, God has the most glorious "instant" of all prepared for His children . . .

Listen, I tell you a mystery: We will not all sleep, but we will all be changed—in a flash, in the twinkling of an eye, at the last trumpet. For the trumpet will sound, the dead will be raised imperishable, and we will be changed.

When the perishable has been clothed with the imperishable, and the mortal with immortality, then the saying that is written will come true: "Death has been swallowed up in victory."

But thanks be to God! He gives us the victory through our Lord Jesus Christ. Therefore, my dear brothers (and sisters), stand firm. Let nothing move you. Always give yourselves fully to the work of the Lord, because you know that your labor in the Lord is not in vain.

—*1 Corinthians 15:51–52, 54, 57–58*

Letter to a Friend

It's our job to introduce our circumstances and feelings to God's resurrection truth.

My *Dear Friend,*

I had such a wonderful time with you the other afternoon, but my heart has been so heavy with your situation and concerns since we talked. I keep praying that God will keep you balanced. You are dealing with so much stress from so many different areas!

It's ironic that I'm in the midst of writing a book about growing through life's storms. When I think of how you're struggling, I am cautioned not to toss out a simplistic challenge to people I've never even met to "trust and *grow* through it all!" (I already felt cautious, but even more so now!)

I know it's not *easy* to trust and look for growth when nothing makes sense—when you're about to lose everything—when there's no peace anywhere—when you feel as if you're the only one in the boat who's rowing. It's all too easy to feel abandoned by an all-powerful, limitless Lord who doesn't appear to be using His power and riches to help when you're clearly going down for the count!

I can't give you (or anyone else) platitudes or easy answers. Because there *are no* easy answers. But I can hold on in faith for you . . . faith in a God of love who won't let us go no matter how bad it looks or feels . . . faith in the work He's doing in you and through you, His beloved child, my dear sister.

And if it does get worse—if God allows you to lose even more that is precious to you—you can be certain that I won't understand or like it any better than you do. I'll probably ask God if He's *sure* this is necessary. I'll probably tell Him you didn't *need* that. I might even get into the subject of what's "fair" and "not fair," like my kids used to do. Because I know that you're doing everything you can possibly do!

But then I'll have to wipe my eyes and go on trusting Him with you. And I'll need to begin praising Him for that hard-to-imagine good that He's *covenanted* to work out for you. Because while *I* don't want to see you *hurting*, I know that *He* won't allow you to be truly *harmed*—even when it hurts and feels like the bottom has dropped out.

May I share one thing with you? When I was carrying you in my heart (everywhere I went the other morning!) I happened to be reading Ray Stedman's book *God's Loving Word.* He was discussing John 19:41–42, which tells us about Joseph of Arimathea and Nicodemus laying Jesus' body in a new tomb in a garden near the place where He was crucified.

Ray writes:

There, in that beautiful garden, just a few yards from the site of Jesus' agony, was this tomb. The cross represented failure and despair.

Certainly, that was the mood of all those who had followed Jesus throughout His earthly ministry, only to see all their hopes nailed to a Roman cross.

But, though Jesus' friends and followers didn't know it then, the place of resurrection was just a few yards from the place of despair and hopelessness. And so it is with you and me.

Perhaps you are feeling a complete bankruptcy of spirit as you read these words. Perhaps you are in a situation which leaves you feeling hopeless. Perhaps, you have been "crucified," unjustly treated by the world around you. Your spirit may be broken, and you see no future ahead of you.

Let me assure you of this: There is a resurrection in your future. You can't see it now, but it is not far away. The empty tomb is near the cross. When you stand close to the cross of Jesus, when you choose to follow the will of God wherever it leads, the Day of Resurrection is just around the corner!

I wait with you, my precious friend. And I hurt and wonder with you. But I also know (as I'm sure some part of you does too) that God has a great "gettin' up mornin'" around the corner for you and your precious family.

That corner just won't come soon enough for either one of us!

I love you, I believe in you, and I'll ride this out with you.

Susan

It is right for me to feel this way about . . . you, since I have you in my heart.   —Philippians 1:7

May our Lord Jesus Christ himself and God our Father, who loved us and by his grace gave us eternal encouragement and good hope, encourage your heart and strengthen you in every good deed and word.

But the Lord is faithful, and he will strengthen and protect you from the evil one. May God direct your heart into God's love and Christ's perseverance.

—2 Thessalonians 2:16–17; 3:3, 5

What a
Life

My grandfather always said that living is like licking honey off a thorn.
Louis Adamic

Life is sweet. It offers sunrises, fat baby fists, darting hummingbirds, commitments, outstretched arms, spring breezes, puppies, giggles, surprise parties, strawberries, voices in harmony, dimples, sheets on a clothesline, curls on little girls, compliments, fresh-baked bread, red wagons, great oak trees, whiskered men, love letters, pink parasols, marching bands, harvest time, feather pillows, waterfalls, boys on bikes, praise songs, full moons, cozy fires, communion, reunion, daisies, helping hands, pounding surf, butterflies, and white clouds mounded in blue skies.

Life is sharp. It pierces with good-byes, fevered brows, screams, empty beds, tornadoes and earthquakes, prejudice, poison ivy, traffic jams, tear-stained cheeks, ignorance, failure, war, drought, explosions, greed, lies, criticism, head-on collisions, rust and rot, floods, doubts, rejection, wrinkles, mosquitoes, hunger, hands that slap or steal, despair, divorce, rape, depression, broken bones, broken promises, broken dreams, broken hearts, broken lives, and dark clouds mounded in gray skies.

How can we enjoy the sweetness of this life without being pricked by its jagged thorns? How can we feel at home in a world blighted by sin yet blessed with the redeeming grace and presence of God?

God's children are not at home here; but we are *here*, nonetheless. And we discover that it's impossible to enjoy this world's sunshine without enduring its clouds and storms. There is no way to withdraw from only one part of life. Resistance to pain inevitably numbs us to joy.

So we accept the reality that this world of clashing darkness and light is where we are required to live and mature. Some day all things will be made new in Christ.

But for now, our job is to stand firm and grow where we are planted by using all the sunshine and rain that comes our way. Would we come to harvest without either?

Jesus told this parable: "The kingdom of heaven is like a man who sowed good seed in his field. But while everyone was sleeping, his enemy came and sowed weeds among the wheat, and went away. When the wheat sprouted and formed heads, then the weeds also appeared.

"The owner's servants came to him and said, 'Sir, didn't you sow good seed in your field? Where then did the weeds come from?'

"'An enemy did this,' he replied. The servants asked him, 'Do you want us to go and pull them up?'

"'No,' he answered, 'because while you are pulling the weeds, you may root up the wheat with them. Let both grow together until the harvest. At that time I will tell the harvesters: First collect the weeds and tie them in bundles to be burned; then gather the wheat and bring it into my barn.'"

—Matthew 13:24–30

Weathering
the Storm

Be still before the LORD and wait patiently for him.

Psalm 37:7

Oh Lord,
let this trouble,
this trial,
cause me to
be still
and know that you are
God.
Use this tension as
surface tension to
hold me,
clinging like a droplet

after a storm,
patiently suspended,
yet holding fast to my
Vine of Life.

The storm swirled, throbbing about my little car as it headed toward the dark mountains. As nature staged the hidden tempest in my soul, my hand moved in rhythm with the windshield wipers doggedly slashing at sliding drops.

Lightning and heartbreak stabbed in jagged flashes. Thunder roared. Leaves and questions tossed wet in the wind.

The torrent poured on before me, yet the sun began to touch and warm my back. A rainbow, soft and wide, embraced the darkest mountain top. "See, I am with you always. I promise, my child. I promise!"

So beautifully God paints understanding and peace with strokes from His own rich palette of promises.

I waited patiently for the LORD; he turned to me and heard my cry. . . . God is our refuge and strength, an ever present help in trouble. Therefore we will not fear, though the earth give way and the mountains fall into the heart of the sea, though its waters roar and foam and the mountains quake with their surging. —Psalm 40:1, 46:1–3

Where can I go from your Spirit? Where can I flee from your presence? If I go up to the heavens, you are there; if I make my bed in the depths, you are there. If I rise on the wings of the dawn, if I settle on the far side of the sea, even there your hand will guide me, your right hand will hold me fast. If I say, "Surely the darkness will hide me and the light become night around me, even the darkness will not be dark to you; the night will shine like the day, for darkness is as light to you.   —Psalm 139:7–1

Seeing Beneath and Beyond

You are looking only on the surface of things.
2 Corinthians 10:7

Looking *at the* surface of life's present circumstances I can come to several conclusions, all of them factual, all of them miserable.

First, I'm being rained on. Again.

Second, I'm soaking wet and shivering in the winds of adversity. Again.

Third, if "wet is wonderful," then I'm more than wonderful because I'm completely and totally *drenched*.

Menacing storms like this one have been lined up on the horizon of my life like a fleet of planes in a relentless landing pattern.

And I can see absolutely no spiritual progress, no

purpose, no good, no gain. From where I stand in the clouds and pouring rain, it's impossible to see what God is doing beneath the surface and beyond the moment.

It *is* possible, however, to *know* without seeing.

Because I know my Heavenly Father. I know He's able to do anything, anywhere, in any weather condition, visibly or invisibly. And whatever He does will always turn out to be good, because *He* is good.

Without seeing, I know that these rains of adversity will soak deep into the soil of who I am and that through it all God will cause me to "take root below and bear fruit above" (2 Kings 19:30). And because of that Root, I will be "filled with the fruit of righteousness that comes through Jesus Christ—to the glory and praise of God" (Philippians 1:11).

God didn't say I should pretend to enjoy this tear-saturated and uncertain landscape. He did say that with eyes of faith I could see *beneath* it to His work within me, and *beyond* it "to the joy set before" me (Hebrews 12:2). . . to the joy set before *us*. He promised His eternal hope for tomorrow, and the grace and peace of His Presence for today.

I'm not alone out in the rain. And neither are you.

We don't yet see things clearly. We're squinting in a fog, peering through a mist. But it won't be long before the weather clears and the sun shines bright! We'll see it all then, see it all as clearly as God sees us, knowing him directly just as he knows us!

—1 Corinthians 13:12, The Message

Now faith is being sure of what we hope for and certain of what we do not see.

Let us fix our eyes on Jesus, the author and perfecter of our faith, who for the joy set before him endured the cross, scorning its shame, and sat down at the right hand of the throne of God. Consider him who endured such opposition from sinful men, so that you will not grow weary and lose heart.

Endure hardship as discipline; God is treating you as sons. For what son is not disciplined by his father? If you are not disciplined (and everyone undergoes discipline), then you are illegitimate children and not true sons. Moreover, we have all had human fathers who disciplined us and we respected them for it. How much more should we submit to the Father of our spirits and live! Our fathers disciplined us for a little while as they thought best; but God disciplines us for our good that we may share in his holiness. No discipline seems pleasant at the time, but painful. Later on, however, it produces a harvest of righteousness and peace for those who have been trained by it. —Hebrews 11:1, 12:2–3, 7–11

A Rich Inheritance

A good man leaves an inheritance for his children's children.

Proverbs 13:22

I *can still barely* believe it, but my Dad is gone. When the emergency room nurse took us to the cubicle where he lay, his arm had slipped and was dangling over the edge of the narrow bed. Instinctively, I reached for his hand. It was cold. Already. Those strong, wonderful hands that were always fixing or building something to help someone, could no longer squeeze back in loving response.

Tears sprang to my eyes as I stood with my sister, brother, and husband, transfixed by the sweeping movement of the second hand on Dad's wristwatch.

Strange that his timepiece should continue to measure the passing minutes when he had just entered a timeless eternity with the Lord. My brother gently slid the watch from his wrist. Time only counted for us.

I took one last good-bye look at his face—ashen now—that used to crinkle into warmth so often. The long sutured welt across the top of his head seemed intrusive—an unnecessary wounding. He was truly gone from his body. And I was truly not ready for this.

When I had left for my speaking trip to Great Britain he was, to all appearances, his usual independent, healthy self. How could a brain tumor have taken him so quickly? When I phoned home (only four days after my previous call) he had already been through surgery and the dreadful diagnosis had been pronounced. Highly malignant. Fast-growing. Terminal. They said he would lose his mind and be totally paralyzed before it was over. Oh, God, please, not like that!

Against great odds my husband and I got an early flight home and I had three precious visits with Dad. Then, mercifully, instantaneously, God took him home. A massive hemorrhage from the site of the tumor. One minute he was sitting in a wheelchair struggling to brush his teeth with the hand that still worked; the next minute he was standing face to face with his wonderful Savior. And he surely stood arm in arm with his beloved wife of more than fifty years, my mother.

The whole thing—diagnosis, surgery, paralysis, prayers for help, and this final answer to prayer—took less than a month from start to finish.

So we buried his body and celebrated his homegoing at a memorial service filled with crying, remembering, rejoicing, holding one another close, and holding one another up.

And now, because I'm committed to writing this book about the blessings God seeks to bring to us through life's storms, I'm trying to figure out what possible gain there could be in such an unexpected, heart-rending tornado of loss as this has been. . . a loss I felt, and continue to feel, deeply.

Certainly I knew that my parents could not always be here—that someday they would die, just as we all will. But the fact is, from my earliest memories Dad always *has* been here. He was the one who taught me to know and love God. He was the rock, the steady, faithful God-honoring head of our family. And he *prayed* for me. Daily, my earthly father had a talk with his Heavenly Father about their daughter. How would I make it without those prayers?

And in the last few years—especially since Mom's death—I had grown used to Dad showing up at our front door with a big bear hug or two and a hankering for some home cooking—a thick slice or two of my honey oatmeal bread accompanied by a steaming bowl of chili, or my slow-simmered pot roast with mashed potatoes and gravy, especially when it was followed by a big wedge of fresh green apple pie, or strawberry shortcake (if the berries were good and sweet). When he came he enjoyed my food, my well-stocked bookshelves, and my company—not necessarily in that order. How would I make it without him and his loving hugs? Where are the *gains* in all these losses?

Could I have gained *appreciation*? Certainly loss deepened it. My father was a good man who had always made me feel secure and loved without saying a word. In his later years, to my great delight, he learned to openly express his affection and to hear and receive my love and appreciation. I'm confident that God is telling him now how very grateful I am for the wonderful, prayerful father He gave me. I'm counting on God to bless him with glories and joys beyond my imagination. So at least Dad has gained a fuller appreciation of my appreciation! (But since heaven is such a happy place, I suspect God won't mention how much I'm missing him.)

Could I also have gained *wisdom and perspective?* I hope so. Psalm 90:12 says, "Teach us to number our days aright, that we may gain a heart of wisdom." Sudden loss reminds us to measure our days, and our struggles, against the backdrop of eternity, for our time on earth is very short. Wisdom encourages us to:

Say love that's unsaid. Now.

Let go of what might keep us apart. Now.

Give while there's a hand to receive. Now.

Hug, laugh, cry, sing, and share our hearts. Now.

For what we dare to give to one another in love enriches us at the time, stays behind to comfort and help at our parting, yet still goes on to heaven—a seed to flower in eternity, bringing perennial joy.

But my biggest gain in this storm of loss is surely my *rich inheritance.* When I spoke at the memorial service I said, "Dad was never wealthy in this world's ways, so

I'm not expecting much of an inheritance in material things from him. In fact, I feel that I've already received my inheritance from Dad."

My brothers and sisters and I do have a valuable inheritance. We were born to a father rich in faith and courage. He remained steadfast, and he prayed, loved, believed, and lived out his hope in Christ. We have inherited an example of faithfulness that can never be taken away. And because Dad "worked at it with all his heart, as working for the Lord, not for men," I know that he "will receive an inheritance from the Lord as a reward" (Colossians 3:23–24.)

We who follow his example will receive the same reward, for our Heavenly Father waits with an unperishable inheritance for those of us who continue to walk in faith and prayer, believing.

Praise be to the God and Father of our Lord Jesus Christ! In his great mercy he has given us new birth into a living hope through the resurrection of Jesus Christ from the dead, and into an inheritance that can never perish, spoil or fade—kept in heaven for you, who through faith are shielded by God's power until the coming of the salvation that is ready to be revealed in the last time. In this you greatly rejoice, though now for a little while you may have had to suffer grief in all kinds of trials. These have come so that your faith—of greater worth than gold, which perishes even though refined by fire—may be proved genuine and may result in praise, glory and honor when Jesus Christ is revealed. Though you have not seen him, you love him; and even though you do not see him now, you believe in him and are filled with an inexpressible and glorious joy, for you are receiving the goal of your faith, the salvation of your souls.

—1 Peter 1:3–9

Rooted by the Storm

I'm prone to
huddle in life's storms,
to crouch 'neath winds and rain.
Should faith unfurl
my cringing soul and
stand me tall in Christ—
what then?
"Whose feet are planted firm in Me,
is rooted by the storm."

Others went out on the sea in ships; they were mer-
chants on the mighty waters. They saw the works of
the LORD, his wonderful deeds in the deep. For he
spoke and stirred up a tempest that lifted high the
waves. They mounted up to the heavens and went

down to the depths; in their peril their courage melted away. They reeled and staggered like drunken men; they were at their wits' end. Then they cried out to the LORD in their trouble, and he brought them out of their distress. He stilled the storm to a whisper; the waves of the sea were hushed.—Psalm 107:23–29

One day he and his disciples got in a boat. "Let's cross the lake," he said. And off they went. It was smooth sailing, and he fell asleep. A terrific storm came up suddenly on the lake. Water poured in, and they were about to capsize. They woke Jesus: "Master, Master, we're going to drown!"

Getting to his feet, he told the wind, "Silence!" and the waves, "Quiet down!" They did it. The lake became smooth as glass.

Then he said to his disciples, "Why can't you trust me?"

They were in absolute awe, staggered and stammering, "Who is this, anyway? He calls out to the winds and sea, and they do what he tells them!"

—Luke 8:22–25, The Message

A Lecture to Myself at Pruning Season

There is no way that we can be effective disciples of Christ except through relentless pruning—the cutting away of non-fruitbearing suckers that sap our energies, but bear no fruit.

Selwyn Hughes, *The Divine Gardener*

Look at you. What a restless branch you are—squirming, aching, offering suggestions, and protesting in the hands of your Lord.

Stop fighting! Stop trying so hard to understand it all, to make the changes, to know the direction and outcome of this pruning.

Rest. Just rest and remain in Him. You know He can be trusted. So trust.

Trust enough to stop trying to be His special assistant. He doesn't need the help. Trust enough to let yourself cry for what is and what isn't. Trust enough to praise and thank your Vine for what is and what will be.

Trust enough to take a nap, for goodness' sake!

"I am the true vine and my Father is the gardener. He cuts off every branch in me that bears no fruit, while every branch that does bear fruit he prunes so that it will be even more fruitful. Remain in me, and I will remain in you. No branch can bear fruit by itself; it must remain in the vine. Neither can you bear fruit unless you remain in me."

John 15:1–2, 4

No discipline seems pleasant at the time, but painful. Later on, however, it produces a harvest of righteousness and peace for those who have been trained by it. —*Hebrews 12:11*

Climbing Through Life's Clutter

If you falter in times of trouble, how small is your strength.

Proverbs 24:10

It's hard to miss those
boulders of trouble that
roll into my life.
They're big enough
to climb on so I
take Your hand, Jesus,
and scramble up with Your help.
It's those pebbles of
pressure,
noise,
and everyday frustration

that are nearly stoning
me senseless.
Lord, toughen my hide and
soften my heart.
Teach me to walk that slow,
winding cobblestone path to
Christian maturity.

So do not throw away your confidence; it will be richly rewarded. You need to persevere so that when you have done the will of God, you will receive what he has promised. For in just a very little while, "He who is coming will come and will not delay. But my righteous one will live by faith. And if he shrinks back, I will not be pleased with him." But we are not of those who shrink back and are destroyed, but of those who believe and are saved.

—Hebrews 10:35–39

Poem reprinted from *When the Handwriting on the Wall Is in Brown Crayon*, copyright © 1981 Susan L. Lenzkes.

When Evil Rains Down

"Whoever serves me must follow me; and where I am, my servant also will be."
John 12:26

I *watch the evening news and squirm as the*
world's soot settles over me,
> *the latest dregs of national gossip,*
> *teeming international inequities,*
> *sordid statistics of greed and compromise,*
> *blatant sin paraded as human rights,*
> *the pollution of violence, oppression, misery.*
I long to escape the debris of this broken world that
> *sifts down*
> *spoiling serenity*
>> *soiling peace and joy.*

Yet dare I close my eyes to the pain that my Lord
*   carried on His back?*
He watched the evening news
*   and staggered to the cross.*

For God so loved the world that he gave his one and
only Son, that whoever believes in him shall not per-
ish but have eternal life. For God did not send his
Son into the world to condemn the world, but to save
the world through him.   —John 3:16–17

You see, at just the right time, when we were still
powerless, Christ died for the ungodly. Very rarely
will anyone die for a righteous man, though for a
good man someone might possibly dare to die. But
God demonstrates his own love for us in this: While
we were still sinners, Christ died for us.

*   For if, when we were God's enemies, we were*
reconciled to him through the death of his Son, how
much more, having been reconciled, shall we be
saved through his life!   —Romans 5:6–8, 10

I tell you, open your eyes and look at the fields!

They are ripe for harvest . . . even now he harvests the crop for eternal life . . . —John 4:35–36

He said to them, "Go into all the world and preach [this] good news to all creation." —Mark 16:15

Let us not become weary in doing good, for at the proper time we will reap a harvest if we do not give up. —Galatians 6:9

To Name a Fear

Who is more foolish, the child afraid of the dark, or the man afraid of the light?
Maurice Freehill

The subject of my Tuesday morning women's Bible study class was fear, and it was with a certain amount of fear that I went off to teach it because I knew I would have to begin with a confession.

While preparing the lesson that week, I had reveled in the satisfaction that I'm not a fearful person. I've never had to wrestle with the vicious lions of fear that I've seen roar through some people's lives and tear them apart.

Just about then the Lord poked His finger through the veneer of my smug attitude, pointing out the sleeping cat that I call Tabby. Instead of dealing with my fear, I made a pet out of it. Instead of conquering it, I patted it on the head and fed it saucers of milk!

How dangerous fear is when it purrs rather than roars. For when we don't recognize it as an enemy we allow it to curl up and stay on the hearth of our lives.

And while claiming that we're not "afraid," we are nevertheless concerned, worried, restless, anxious, bored, frequently sick, and unmotivated (or else working frantically). Or we feel guilty, indecisive, possessive, defensive, negative, shy, or tired—oh, so tired!

It takes a brave person to admit, "I'm worried because I'm afraid you'll . . ." "I can't choose because I fear that if . . ." "I'm so tired from working hard to prevent . . ." "I feel vulnerable when . . ." "But what if . . ."

The masks of fear are many and varied. They need to be uncovered and exposed to the Light of the World, Who says, "Fear not!" For He knows how many things in this world evoke fear in His children.

When we're ready to call our fear by its first name, we're ready to receive Jesus' antidote to fear—which is simply (or sometimes not so simply) the faith to trust in Him. He is able.

Then he placed his right hand on me and said: "Do not be afraid. I am the Living One; I was dead, and behold I am alive for ever and ever!"

—Revelation 1:17–18

The LORD is my light and my salvation—whom shall I fear? The LORD is the stronghold of my life— of whom shall I be afraid? When evil men advance against me to devour my flesh, when my enemies and my foes attack me, they will stumble and fall. Though an army besiege me, even then will I be confident. For in the day of trouble he will keep me safe in his dwelling; he will hide me in the shelter of his tabernacle and set me high upon a rock.

—Psalm 27:1–3, 5

I sought the LORD, and he answered me; he delivered me from all my fears. Those who look to him are radiant; their faces are never covered with shame.

—Psalm 34:4–5

Daily
Sprinkles

I *want to grow, Lord.*
It's all right with me
if You send some trial my way
so I'll learn to lean on Your strength.
Don't spare me by making it small—
send a big Biblical blast of
holy refining fire.
Don't let my bickering children,
this tension headache,
the incessantly ringing telephone,
these broken dishes,
this draining tiredness,
the heat and smog
or these boring repetitive tasks
distract me—

so that when a trial comes
I miss it.
It would be such a shame
if I overlooked my chance
to grow closer to You!

You let the distress bring you to God, not drive you from him. The result was all gain, no loss.

Distress that drives us to God does that. It turns us around. It gets us back in the way of salvation. We never regret that kind of pain. But those who let distress drive them away from God are full of regrets, end up on a deathbed of regrets.

And now, isn't it wonderful all the ways in which this distress has goaded you closer to God? You're more alive, more concerned, more sensitive, more reverent, more human, more passionate, more responsible. Looked at from any angle, you've come out of this with purity of heart.

—2 Corinthians 7:9–11, The Message

I'm Not Good Enough

One does not sow and reap in the same day.
John Claypool

One of life's biggest discouragements is the disparity between the high plain for which my soul cries out and the valley where I generally plow my crooked furrows. Over the years I have often brought to the Lord my need to do better than I do and be better than I am.

There is nothing wrong with stretching for the best, with reaching toward the perfection that will one day be our inheritance. Even the Apostle Paul must have felt this way for he said, "Not that I have already obtained all this, or have already been made perfect, but I press on to take hold of that for which Christ Jesus took hold of me" (Philippians 3:12).

The trouble begins not when I obediently and faithfully press on toward the goal of being made perfect in Christ; it begins when I am a perfectionist. A perfectionist resists the truth that growing up in Christ is a process. After all, we read the Bible and we know what He intends us to be. So we should be that way now. Such thinking creates its own storms and difficulties.

We struggle so hard to achieve perfection that we become exhausted and joyless. We fail to own or appreciate our humanity, even though God has declared His chosen dwelling place to be with us, just as we are.

All this creates an even bigger problem. As perfectionists we find it difficult, if not impossible, to believe that God could completely accept, love, and long to be with us in this unfinished state. We speak of His love and freedom, but we don't rest in it.

We allowed God's grace to save us, but somehow it doesn't seem enough to keep us (though we would never actually say that). We say "God's grace is sufficient for us" but we act as if grace is given to strengthen our efforts to earn His love. Such deeply imbedded attitudes isolate us in a prison of endless striving and eventual despair.

Peace comes only when we acknowledge that human effort cannot sustain righteousness any more than it could create it. God's truth waits to set us free as we acknowledge that our most disciplined effort can create only an image, a mere picture, of righteousness. And we all know that even the most beautiful picture of a tree can produce no real fruit.

Our Heavenly Gardener waits for access to the earthy loam of our life and heart—as we are today. Only then can He begin to plow, plant, and nourish His seeds of true and lasting righteousness.

Let me put this question to you: how did your new life begin? Was it by working your heads off to please God? Or was it by responding to God's Message to you? Are you going to continue this craziness? For only crazy people would think they could complete by their own efforts what was begun by God. If you weren't smart enough or strong enough to begin it, how do you suppose you could perfect it? Did you go through this whole painful learning process for nothing? —Galatians 3:3–4, The Message

The former regulation is set aside because it was weak and useless (for the law made nothing perfect), and a better hope is introduced, by which we draw near to God. Therefore [Jesus Christ] is able to save completely those who come to God through him, because he always lives to intercede for them. Such a high priest meets our need—one who is holy, blameless, pure, set apart from sinners, exalted above the heavens. Because by one sacrifice he has made perfect forever those who are being made holy.

—Hebrews 7:18, 25–26; 10:14

Continue to work out your salvation with fear and trembling, for it is God who works in you to will and to act according to his good purpose.

—Philippians 2:12–13

So neither he who plants nor he who waters is anything, but only God, who makes things grow.

—1 Corinthians 3:7

Cultivating Joy

What has happened to all your joy?
Galatians 4:15

Through His great and
precious promises,
God generously sprinkles
His seeds of joy in our hearts.
Yet too often we reap a
harvest of misery.
Joy's seed
requires deep furrows of faith,
sprouts in the rich soil of trust,
is nourished by daily
soaking in God's Word,
blossoms in eager response to

His love,
grows strong through
winds of adversity,
and bears fruit only as we
stay rooted in obedience to
Christ's commands.
And how true that
the tender seedling of
God's joy
and the stubborn weed of
self-pity
cannot survive in the same garden!

Joy is not mere happiness. Nor does joy spring from a life of ease, comfort, or peaceful circumstances. Joy is the soul's buoyant response to a God of promise, presence, and power.

Joy lifts our spirit above earth's sorrow, dancing in jubilation at the hope set before us. Joy is faith feasting and celebrating the One in Whom it trusts. Joy is the heart vibrating in grateful rhythm to the love of Almighty God who actually chooses to make His home within us. Joy is the child of God reclining in the luxury of a Father

Who is "able to do immeasurably more than all we ask or imagine according to his power that is at work within us" (Ephesians 3:20).

Joy is the vine-ripened fruit grown of God's own Spirit Who is at work within us as we trust and obey— and it is sweet to both God and man.

The fruit of the Spirit is love, joy . . .
—Galatians 5:22

If you obey my commands, you will remain in my love, just as I have obeyed my Father's commands and remain in his love. I have told you this so that my joy may be in you and that your joy may be complete. *—John 15:10–11*

As the rain and the snow come down from heaven, and do not return to it without watering the earth and making it bud and flourish, so that it yields seed for the sower and bread for the eater, so is my word that goes out from my mouth: It will not return to me empty, but will accomplish what I desire and achieve the purpose for which I sent it. You will go out in joy and be led forth in peace: the mountains and hills will burst into song before you, and all the trees of the field will clap their hands.

—Isaiah 55:10–12

The desert and the parched land will be glad; the wilderness will rejoice and blossom. Like the crocus, it will burst into bloom; it will rejoice greatly and shout for joy. Gladness and joy will overtake them, and sorrow and sighing will flee away.

—Isaiah 35:1–2, 10

For the LORD your God will bless you in all your harvest and in all the work of your hands, and your joy will be complete.   —Deuteronomy 16:15

Melting Boredom

A rut is a grave with the ends knocked out.
Laurence J. Peter

Boredom *was smothering* me in the orange heat of that long ago afternoon when my little boy rushed in with his announcement. "I know how to catch a moth now, Mommy!" To demonstrate he stalked, straddle-legged, across the kitchen floor, elbows flung out, hands perched to pounce. "And then you grab him. Like this!" And he attacked a spot on the floor with his powerful five-year-old pincher grip.

"I see," I said, amused. "That looks pretty good. But moths are hard to catch. They have wings—you don't!"

"I can do it, don't worry."

"Well, what if you do catch one?" I continued,

determined to confound this seemingly impossible plan before it disappointed him. "How will you feed it? What do moths like to eat?"

"Oh, flowers, I guess."

So he spent all afternoon filling plastic sandwich bags with one surprised moth and one small yellow marigold each. I spent all afternoon learning that boredom is candle wax beneath the flaming wick of enthusiasm. And I began to understand something else, too.

When we allow ourselves to become bored, when we lose our sense of adventure, we grow *older* but not *wiser*. Wisdom enlarges our capacity for discovery and delight, causing wonder to grow as we grow.

We'll spend eternity exploring and rejoicing in the unsearchable riches of God's character, purpose, love, Living Word, and astounding creativity. We need to begin on this earth. What a joy to catch the wonder of God's work around us, and *in* us!

Open my eyes that I may see wonderful things. . . .
I am a stranger on earth; . . . To all perfection I see
a limit; but your commands are boundless.
—Psalm 119:18-19, 96

Great is the LORD and most worthy of praise: his greatness no one can fathom. One generation will commend your works to another; they will tell of your mighty acts. They will speak of the glorious splendor of your majesty, and I will meditate on your wonderful works. They will celebrate your abundant goodness and sing of your righteousness.

—Psalm 145:3–5, 7

The secret things belong to the LORD our God, but the things revealed belong to us and to our children forever . . .   *—Deuteronomy 29:29*

At that time Jesus said, "I praise you, Father, Lord of heaven and earth, because you have hidden these things from the wise and learned, and revealed them to little children. Yes, Father, for this was your good pleasure.   *—Matthew 11:25–26*

New
Beginnings

**The best thing about the future is that it
comes only one day at a time.**
Abraham Lincoln

The beginning of a new year—always an experience in
tentative hope! Those midnight chimes that ring out
the old year and bring in the new seem to chant, "What
lies ahead?"

And feeling both fear and trust within us, we grope
to join hands in fortress against the unknown. Secret
dreads chip away the edges of new chances. Precious
ties dangle loosely. Clocks tick ever faster.

Yet pushing up through our apprehension like a
crocus through snow is the bright delight of opportunity. For there sits that calendar, fresh and yawning to

be filled with dreams achieved and goals attained. And there stands our Lord saying, "Fear not, just follow Me. I am the same yesterday, today, and forever" (see Hebrews 13:8).

When times are good, be happy; but when times are bad, consider: God has made the one as well as the other. Therefore, a man cannot discover anything about his future. —Ecclesiastes 7:14

"For I know the plans I have for you," declares the LORD, "plans to prosper you and not to harm you, plans to give you hope and a future." —Jeremiah 29:11

Since you are my rock and my fortress, for the sake of your name lead and guide me. . . . I trust in you, O LORD. I say, "You are my God." My times are in your hands. . . . —Psalm 31:3, 14–15

Jesus . . . said, "I am the light of the world. Whoever follows me will never walk in darkness, but will have the light of life." —John 8:12

Trust

Blessed is the man who trusts in the LORD, whose trust is the LORD.
Jeremiah 17:7 RSV

Stoop-shouldered,
foot-dragging,
sighing
resignation
is not trust.
Real trust
bounces on eager toes of
anticipation—
laughs with the pure delight
of knowing
in whom it believes—
rests easy
knowing

on whom it waits.
Lord,
so wrap me in the
knowledge of You
that my trust is no longer
in You, but
is You.

Children are cutest when no one's watching—or they think no one is.

I had just stepped into the kitchen with an armload of laundry when the sight of our boys standing together on the back step caught my eye. Their backs were turned, so they didn't see me looking as the little one wrapped his arm around his brother's knees and tilted his blond head back, gazing up. He barely reached his brother's belt loops.

In a tiny voice he said, "Bend your ear down a minute—I want to tell you a secret."

Then, very quietly, he whispered something that delighted them both.

You know, Jesus, I can't help thinking as I watch them . . . after all these years of walking with You, I still don't even stretch to Your knees. Bend Your ear down a minute, I want to tell You a secret. I think You're wonderful. And I really do trust You. When I grow up I want to be just like You.

Blessed is the man [woman] who makes the LORD his [her] trust. —Psalm 40:4

For you have been my hope, O Sovereign LORD, my confidence since my youth. From birth I have relied on you; you brought me forth from my mother's womb. I will ever praise you. Since my youth, O God, you have taught me, and to this day I declare your marvelous deeds. Even when I am old and gray, do not forsake me, O God, till I declare your power to the next generation, your might to all who are to come. —Psalm 71:5–6, 17–18

I will say of the LORD, "He is my refuge and my fortress, my God, in whom I trust." —Psalm 91:2

Five Ways to Handle Fear and Worry

Worry does not empty tomorrow of its sorrow, it empties today of its strength.
Corrie ten Boom

I once knew someone so
simple-minded and unaware
that fear never entered her world.
Worry never invaded her innocence.
Ignorance became bliss.

I once knew someone so
informed and educated
that future fears stalked her world.
Worry endlessly postulated doom.
Intelligence became dread.

I once knew someone so
idealistic and spiritual
that fear was denied.
Worry disguised itself as repetitious prayers.
Ideology became escapism.

I once knew someone so
capable and determined
that fear was a challenge to avoid disaster.
Worry simply required more work.
Intervention became exhaustion.

I once knew someone so
realistic and wise
that she feared and trusted only God.
This world's worries were placed in His hands.
Inability became peace.

"And he asked them, 'Why were you so fearful?
Don't you even yet have confidence in me?'"
—Jesus Christ, Mark 4:40 TLB

"I tell you, my friends, do not be afraid of those who

kill the body and after that can do no more. But I will show you whom you should fear: Fear him who, after the killing of the body, has the power to throw you into hell. Yes, I tell you, fear him. Are not five sparrows sold for two pennies? Yet not one of them is forgotten by God. Indeed, the very hairs of your head are all numbered. Don't be afraid; you are worth more than many sparrows."

—Luke 12:4–7

There is no fear in love. But perfect love drives out fear, because fear has to do with punishment. The one who fears is not made perfect in love. We love because he first loved us. *—1 John 4:18–19*

Cast all your anxiety on him because he cares for you. *—1 Peter 5:7*

God has said, "Never will I leave you; never will I forsake you." So we say with confidence, "The Lord is my helper; I will not be afraid. What can man do to me?" *—Hebrews 13:5–6*

Walking While Waiting

With your help I can advance . . .
2 Samuel 22:30

Sometimes we are certain that we're going nowhere in life. We are trapped between the walls of some narrow, spartan place that we're sure must be one of life's dreary waiting rooms. So we sit down, reach for an outdated periodical, and wait for someone to open a door and call our name.

Many of us who think we are being patient may actually be camping out in one of life's hallways! Our Lord's house has many rooms, and how can we get from one to another except through a hallway? Yes, some are long, some narrow, some dark, and some cold. Yet if we fail to understand the purpose of a hallway, we're likely to wander about for years, assuming we are "waiting on the Lord."

Life's hallways *are* places of transition even though we see no change. And because God is with us, such places offer our finest progress.

When faith holds out a hand to God in the dark, we're already *there* even though we haven't yet *arrived*. Waiting on God is the same as walking with God toward exciting new rooms of potential and service.

But we can't see progress in a dark hallway. And although we don't like being stuck there without a flashlight, few other places are so quiet and devoid of outside distractions.

Windowless halls can be the perfect place to discover God and His quiet grace. They are places where time seems to stand still and so we stop and give names to our deepest needs and then give them up to God's care and timing.

On days when we're feeling tired or hopelessly lost, He carries us in His arms. At other times He waits until we grope for His hand and begin to follow along, learning to walk by *faith*, not by *sight*.

When we finally arrive at the door that swings

open into the light, we realize that our Heavenly Father can see perfectly well in the dark. We can trust Him to bring us to the next door in His perfect time—the time that will most benefit us and the glory of His name.

Let's practice waiting on the Lord even as we faithfully walk the narrow way.

Let your eyes look straight ahead, fix your gaze directly before you. Make level paths for your feet and take only ways that are firm. Do not swerve to the right or the left; keep your foot from evil.
—Proverbs 4:25–27

But one thing I do: Forgetting what is behind and straining toward what is ahead, I press on toward the goal to win the prize for which God has called me heavenward in Christ Jesus. All of us who are mature should take such a view of things.
—Philippians 3:14–15

Rejoice in the Lord always. I will say it again: Rejoice! Let your gentleness be evident to all. The Lord is near. Do not be anxious about anything, but in everything, by prayer and petition, with thanks-giving, present your requests to God. And the peace of God, which transcends all understanding, will guard your hearts and your minds in Christ Jesus. For I have learned to be content whatever the cir-cumstances. I can do everything through him who gives me strength. —Philippians 4:4–7, 11, 13

You are my lamp, O LORD; the LORD turns my darkness into light. It is God who arms me with strength and makes my way perfect. You broaden the path beneath me, so that my ankles do not turn.
—2 Samuel 22:29, 33, 37

God's Exchange System

To all who mourn . . . he will give: Beauty for ashes; Joy instead of mourning; Praise instead of heaviness.

Isaiah 61:3 LB

Whenever *we bow* in real understanding before our Lord—whether it's at the cradle, the cross, or the empty tomb; whether we're seeing Him as Savior, Friend, or conquering King—we will long to give Him some wonderful, worthy gift. The Eastern Wise Men brought gold, frankincense, and myrrh!

But we know how it is, how it has always been. We come to Him dressed in the rags of sin—and He gives us His robe of righteousness. We offer our empty, broken hearts—and He fills them with healing love.

We bring Him needs—He supplies His endless resources. We give tears—He gives comfort. We give weakness—He gives grace. We cry out our fears and questions—He whispers His peace and purpose. We present ignorance wrapped in pride—He returns wisdom wrapped in humility.

He knows how it is, how it has always been, and yet He pleads with us to continue to come to Him and give all that we are and all that we are not.

Because He knows something else. He knows that when we have finally given Him all that we are and have received all that He is, we will at last hold the One Gift worth giving away.

Our gold is surrender; our frankincense, praise; our myrrh, loving obedience to His command to give as generously as He has given unto us. He receives such gifts with joy.

Does the LORD delight in burnt offerings and sacri-
fices as much as in obeying the voice of the LORD?
To obey is better than sacrifice, and to heed than the
fat of rams.   —1 Samuel 15:22

Through Jesus, therefore, let us continually offer to God a sacrifice of praise—the fruit of lips that confess his name. And do not forget to do good and to share with others, for with such sacrifices God is pleased. —Hebrews 13:15–16

We know that we have come to know him if we obey his commands. If anyone obeys his word, God's love is truly made complete in him. This is how we know we are in him: Whoever claims to live in him must walk as Jesus did. —1 John 2:3, 5–6

"Give, and it will be given to you. A good measure, pressed down, shaken together and running over, will be poured into your lap. For with the measure you use, it will be measured to you."

—Luke 6:38

I have neither silver nor gold, but I will give you what I have. —Acts 3:6 MLB

Free from Misconceptions

Stand fast therefore in the liberty by which Christ has made us free, and do not be entangled again . . .

Galatians 5:1 NKJV

What daily doings—
  and undoings—
loosen the laces of
  our shiny Sunday shoes of
  certainty about God and His ways?
We learned to tie them—
  so proud—
  practicing carefully,
  seeking smiles.
But when life's riddles and pain begin to

work loose those
securely tugged knots that assured us
of an easy, predictable life with God,
when we trip on our
trailing laces
and sit looking at their
frayed and soiled ends;
when we can't keep things
all tied up anymore,
dare we step out of our familiar
shiny "pat answers" to
walk on in Truth's barefoot freedom?
For our God is neither
simple nor manageable,
but He is
loving and trustworthy.

Your righteousness reaches to the skies, O God, you who have done great things. Who, O God, is like you? Though you have made me see troubles, many and bitter, you will restore my life again; from the depths of the earth you will again bring me up. You will increase my honor and comfort me once again. I will praise you with the harp for your faithfulness, O my God; I will sing praise to you with the lyre, O Holy One of Israel. My lips will shout for joy when I sing praise to you—I, whom you have redeemed.

—Psalm 71:19–23

Who's Hurting Now?

Jesus,
*I'll know who's
    number one
    if I count the
    tears.
Have I shed more
    for your grief,
    or mine?*

When life is difficult, we might try setting aside our own
pain and ask God what hurts Him. Does it hurt Him
when He shows us the beauty of His light and we turn
away toward darkness? When He fits us with the spec-
tacles of His heavenly view and we grope myopically?
When He offers uncommon guidance and we follow

our own common sense? When He shows us *the* Way and we are content to take *any old* way?

Do His eyes get misty when He spreads a banquet of love before us and we pass it up to nibble on the dry crumbs of hate and resentment? When He offers power to move mountains and we stumble over dirt clods? When He delivers us from evil and we wink at His Enemy? When we cling to Him in pain and then wave to Him in ease? When He presents peace and we battle over it? When He offers salvation to all and we hoard it as a private joy? When we cry out to Him to save us but refuse to live in the safety of His presence?

He waits to help in our weakness, sin, and failure. He already shared *our* pain. When we begin to understand *His* pain, growth begins.

"For my thoughts are not your thoughts, neither are your ways my ways," declares the LORD. "As the heavens are higher than the earth, so are my ways higher than your ways and my thoughts then your thoughts." —Isaiah 55:8–9

God looks down from heaven on the sons (and

daughters) of men to see if there are any who understand, any who seek God. Will the evildoers never
learn—those who . . . do not call on God? There
they were, overwhelmed with dread, where there
was nothing to dread.   —Psalm 53:2, 4–5

Teach me your way, O LORD, and I will walk in
your truth; give me an undivided heart that I may
fear your name. I will praise you, O LORD my God,
with all my heart; I will glorify your name forever.
For great is your love toward me.

—Psalm 86:11–13

I will instruct you and teach you in the way you
should go; I will counsel you and watch over you.
Do not be like the horse or the mule, which have no
understanding but must be controlled by bit and bri-
dle or they will not come to you. Many are the woes
of the wicked, but the LORD's unfailing love sur-
rounds the man (woman) who trusts in him. Rejoice
in the LORD and be glad, you righteous; sing, all you
who are upright in heart!   —Psalm 32:8–11

"Your fruitfulness comes from me." Who is wise? He will realize these things. Who is discerning? He will understand them. The ways of the LORD are right; and the righteous walk in them, but the rebellious stumble in them. —Hosea 14:8–9

Perspectives on Pain

What do people mean when they say "I am not afraid of God because I know He is good?" Have they never even been to a dentist?

C. S. Lewis

C. S. Lewis had a great mind and a great faith, both of which were shaped on the anvil of living and loving in this broken world. He was a realist. And he was honest. He permitted the questions that pain brings. I suspect he had learned that faith speaks loudest to fears that are faced.

When he and his beloved wife, Joy, were dealing with her terminal illness, he commented to a friend in a letter, "We are not necessarily doubting that God will do the best for us; we are wondering how painful the best will turn out to be."

My husband and I are wondering the same thing. Recently Herb was told his cancer is active again—the doctor mentioned it only a few days before his body began to spread the painful news. He has now begun treatment with an experimental drug that we pray God will use to bring him back into remission—a rarity at this stage of his illness. So we don't really know what God has ahead for us. We are living by faith in a hailstorm of uncertainty.

Our visibility is hampered in these weather conditions. It's easy to see misery and need—they are right in front of our eyes. Pain medications are increasing, and Herb is moving with greater difficulty. But to see through this storm to a future and a hope is more difficult. Through tears, we strain to see God's goodness and purpose.

How thankful we are that, long before these dark clouds gathered, the Apostle Paul prayed for our vision problem. His words are recorded in Ephesians 1:18–19: "I pray also that the eyes of your heart may be enlightened in order that you may know the hope to which he has called you, the riches of his glorious inheritance in the saints, and his incomparably great power for us who believe."

A light to cut through the darkness of this earth's storms? Eyes to see hope in a seemingly hopeless situation? A rich inheritance that's not way out there somewhere, lost in the dark? And God's great power, right here, right now, waiting to act on my behalf, waiting to be believed?

So "hope," and the "riches of Christ," and the "power of God" come as we are huddled in our corner of heartache. And we are comforted, yes, but we also gain perspective. Such perspective keeps us from blaming God for bringing this trouble to us. It keeps us from focusing on our fear of the pain. Instead it allows us to begin to praise Him for using this trouble for our good and His glory, even if we never see it on this earth. It helps us to trust His purpose in the midst.

All of this is true, and it sounds so good in the daylight when I'm writing about the realities of life as a child of God. But at midnight—and it's midnight now—it hurts to believe the truth. I want to call up a friend and say, "Can any of this actually be right? It just doesn't seem fair! This dear man who has been my strength shouldn't have to be suffering; he shouldn't be struggling to stand, or jerking in his sleep like this. Can this frightening disease actually be allowed in God's plan? And is God with us now in this room, surrounding and caring for us as I cry while my husband sleeps fitfully?"

Yes, He's here now.

And I find a certainty gripping me—a deep knowledge: God doesn't waste anything. Not doubts or rain; not suffering or pain.

From the suffering of His Son, He produced salvation. He leaves it to us to prove what He will create if we trust Him through our pain.

In our hearts we felt the sentence of death. But this happened that we might not rely on ourselves but on God, who raises the dead. He has delivered us from such a deadly peril, and he will deliver us. On him we have set our hope that he will continue to deliver us, as you help us by your prayers. Then many will give thanks on our behalf for the gracious favor granted us in answer to the prayers of many. . . .

Now it is God who makes both us and you stand firm in Christ. He anointed us, set his seal of ownership on us, and put his Spirit in our hearts as a deposit guaranteeing what is to come.

—2 Corinthians 1:9–11, 21–22

I consider that our present sufferings are not worth comparing with the glory that will be revealed in us.

—Romans 8:18

He Still Lights the Darkness

The people living in darkness have seen a great light; . . . on those living in the land of the shadow of death a light has dawned.
Isaiah 9:2, Matthew 4:16

*What was December twenty-fifth
before it was Christmas?
Just a chilly day
twenty-five sighs into an
endless winter night.
But when it became Christmas—
oh, when it became Christmas
it glowed!*

A star, *radiant and* compelling, announced Christ's birth. Yet it could not have been easy to find that baby beneath its beam and realize that here was the resplendent miracle of the ages—that this Newborn's cry was the brilliant cry of salvation. For the Light of the World slid into our darkness with a whimper and a need to suck. Nothing regal here.

How astounding to enter that stable and realize that Almighty God had dared to pour all of Himself into dimpled arms and legs to be held in the arms of His creation. Perhaps God knew that if we could recognize and reach out for Him first in this dark unlikely barn, we would go on finding Him in life's dark unlikely days. He still comes to light our darkness.

It started when God said, "Light up the darkness!" and our lives filled up with light as we saw and understood God in the face of Christ, all bright and beautiful.   —2 Corinthians 4:6, The Message

Arise, shine, for your light has come, and the glory of the LORD rises upon you. See, darkness covers the earth and thick darkness is over the peoples, but the

LORD rises upon you and his glory appears over you. Nations will come to your light, and kings to the brightness of your dawn.

The sun will no more be your light by day, nor will the brightness of the moon shine on you, for the LORD will be your everlasting light, and your God will be your glory. Your sun will never set again, and your moon will wane no more; the LORD will be your everlasting light, and your days of sorrow will end. —Isaiah 60:1–3, 19–20

"I, the LORD, have called you in righteousness; I will take hold of your hand. I will keep you and will make you to be a covenant for the people and a light for the Gentiles, to open eyes that are blind, and to free captives from prison and to release from the dungeon those who sit in darkness."
—Isaiah 42:6–7

This is how God showed his love among us: He sent his one and only Son into the world that we might live through him. —1 John 4:9

Through him all things were made; without him nothing was made that has been made. In him was life, and that life was the light of men. The light shines in the darkness, but the darkness has not understood it. —John 1:3–5

Who is it that overcomes the world? Only he who believes that Jesus is the Son of God. And this is the testimony; God has given us eternal life, and this life is in his Son. He who has the Son has life, he who does not have the Son of God does not have life. —1 John 5:5, 11–12

Soaring in His Image

Therefore, if anyone is in Christ, he is a new creation; the old has gone, the new has come!
2 Corinthians 5:17

Every day I watch hawks sweeping through the canyon outside my window, taking advantage of invisible hills and valleys of wind that allow them to soar. How magnificent they are! How true to their Creator's intention!

As I watch them, I pray, "Father, make me that free and alive. Keep me from scurrying about the underbrush when I could have a place on the lofty currents that pass empty overhead. I waste so much power when I huddle or crawl. I miss seeing so much beauty when I play the role of rodent, burrowing, hiding, and hoarding. You offer me so much—so much mercy for sin, so much grace for living, so much strength for weakness. What is the untested wingspan of Your purpose in me? Oh, Lord, if I do nothing else in my life, may I at least honor You by being, doing, and enjoying what You created me to be, do, and enjoy. Let me soar!"

You were taught, with regard to your former way of life, to put off your old self, which is being corrupted by its deceitful desires; to be made new in the attitude of your minds; and to put on the new self, created to be like God in true righteousness and holiness. —Ephesians 4:22–24

Do you not know? Have you not heard? The LORD is the everlasting God, the Creator of the ends of the earth. He will not grow tired or weary, and his understanding no one can fathom. He gives strength to the weary and increases the power of the weak. Even youths grow tired and weary, and young men stumble and fall; but those who hope in the LORD will renew their strength. They will soar on wings like eagles; they will run and not grow weary, they will walk and not be faint. —Isaiah 40:28–31

Going Deeper

He said, "Put out into deep water and let down the nets for a catch."

Jesus Christ, Luke 5:4

Lord,
*It's beginning to seem crowded here
in the shallows where I've always
joyfully splashed in the
waters of salvation,
cooling myself with Your promises,
sipping the waters of grace
from Your hand—
quenching my light thirst.
My thirst is greater now
and yearning toward the deep.*

But how I fear
going in over my head!
People drown out there—
die to self—
totally immersed in the mighty
flood of Your righteousness.
Have You made me
dissatisfied, Lord?
Are you,
drawing me
into Your holy depths?
Help me move toward You
in childlike trust, oh
Deep and Living Water!

As the deer pants for streams of water, so my soul
pants for you, O God. My soul thirsts for God, for
the living God. Where can I go and meet with God?
Deep calls to deep in the roar of your waterfalls; all
your waves and breakers have swept over me.

—Psalm 42:1–2, 7

You've had a taste of God. Now, like infants at the

breast, drink deep of God's pure kindness. Then you'll grow up mature and whole in God. . . . As obedient children, let yourselves be pulled into a way of life shaped by God's life, a life energetic and blazing with holiness. God said, "I am holy; you be holy." —1 Peter 2:2; 1:14–16, The Message

"Come, all you who are thirsty, come to the waters . . ." —Isaiah 55:1

Therefore let us leave the elementary teachings about Christ and go on to maturity. —Hebrews 6:1

Lord of
the Valleys

I am . . . a lily of the valley.
Song of Songs 2:1

Very early in life I discovered, much to my delight, that the name *Susan* means "lily." As a representative of such a lovely flower I felt obligated each spring to buy myself a potted lily, watch it bloom, and breathe deeply as it released its sweet scent. This was an enjoyable little private ritual—until a couple of friends educated me as to the true meaning of my name.

While walking with me through my most recent string of trials, testing, and attacks from the enemy, these two friends decided separately to encourage me with one of those small gift cards that tells the meaning of a person's name and cites an appropriate verse of scripture. The verse and picture on each of the cards was different, but the meaning given for my name was the same. Surprisingly, however, the flower my name comes from is not "Lily" but "Lily of the Valley." Oh my.

Perhaps that helps to explain things of late. I'm not the lily I thought I was. If I had known about the "valley clause" I might have changed my name before it was too late!

This is a lily of an entirely different sort. Fragrant and lovely, yes, but it grows its cascade of tiny bell-like blooms in the lowlands—down in the valleys of life. No mountaintop vistas for this little beauty.

It's easy for those of us who are "valley-dwellers" to feel lost down here in life's shaded ravines—swamped by the rain that so often falls here. At times we feel hidden from God's attention, care, and help, especially when we're being pelted by torrential downpours. But when our Lord declared, "I am with you always" (Matthew 28:20), His promise included those of us planted in the bottomlands, depressions, and gullies of life. He is here to help us grow strong in the face of all that comes to us, for He declares Himself to be not only the

God of the mountaintops, but also the God of the valleys.

As proof of this, He led me to a remarkable passage in 1 Kings 20, which tells the story of Israel being threatened by the vast Aramean forces in the hills outside Samaria. We who are weak and besieged are encouraged to realize how God enabled the relatively small armies of Ahab, king of Israel, to defeat the vast Aramean armies led by King Aram and the thirty-two kings allied with him.

Then, even though God had given Israel the victory in this battle, He continued to take thoughtful care of His people by warning them to fortify for another attack from the Arameans the following spring (vv. 13–22).

Meanwhile, the Arameans thought they knew why they had been overpowered. They had fought in the hills, and they figured that Israel's high and holy "god of the hills" could easily protect them in such places! So they decided to wage war on the plains where "surely we will be stronger than they" (v. 25).

So in the spring the Arameans confidently covered the countryside with their troops, looking scornfully across at the Israelites camped opposite them "like two small flocks of goats" (v. 27). It must have been quite a scene. But God had another surprise for them.

As God's people stood in the valley, probably overwhelmed by the odds facing them, God said to them: "Because the Arameans think the Lord is a god of the hills and not a god of the valleys, I will deliver this vast army into your hands, and you will know that I am the Lord" (v. 28).

Thank you, mighty Lord of the Valleys. It's not so bad being a lily of the valley with You here to protect me.

Even though I walk through the valley of the shadow of death, I will fear no evil, for you are with me, your rod and your staff, they comfort me. You prepare a table before me in the presence of my enemies.
—Psalm 23:4–5

"So do not fear, for I am with you; do not be dismayed, for I am your God. I will strengthen you and help you; I will uphold you with my righteous right hand. All who rage against you will surely be

ashamed and disgraced; those who oppose you will be as nothing and perish. Though you search for your enemies, you will not find them. Those who wage war against you will be nothing at all. For I am the Lord, your God, who takes hold of your right hand and says to you, Do not fear; I will help you.

"I will make . . . springs within the valleys."

Isaiah 41:10–13, 18

Safe on Top
of Everything

Whoever trusts in the LORD is kept safe.
Proverbs 29:25

When wicked men would not repent,
God's rain of judgment soon was sent.
So God said, "Noah build a boat,
an ark of promise that will float
above the flood and let you sing,
safe on top of everything."

When heartaches rain from heavy skies,
and troubled waters round me rise,
then I will build a place to hide.
Upon God's promise I will ride
on storm-tossed seas until I sing,

safe on top of everything.

As evil reigned in Noah's day
it will again, but we won't stay!
God promised that if we abide
in the Ark of Christ, one day we'll rise
above this world and forever sing,
safe on top of everything!*

"Oh, that I had the wings of a dove! I would fly
away and be at rest. I would hurry to my place of
shelter, far from the tempest and storm."
—Psalm 55: 6, 8

For in the day of trouble he will keep me safe in his
dwelling; he will hide me in the shelter of his taberna-
cle and set me high upon a rock.   —Psalm 27:5

If you fully obey the LORD your God and carefully
follow all his commands I give you today, the LORD
your God will set you high above all the nations on
earth. . . you will always be at the top, never at the
bottom.   —Deuteronomy 28:1, 13

O LORD, you are my God; I will exalt you and praise your name, for in perfect faithfulness you have done marvelous things, things planned long ago. You have been a refuge for the poor, a refuge for the needy in his distress, a shelter from the storm.
—Isaiah 25:1, 4

* Special thanks to Mary A. Myers for permitting me to use the lovely progression of thought from her poem (of the same title), rewriting it into a song. The verses to that song appear here. Mary is a precious eighty-six-year-old sister in Christ who has "adopted me" across a continent, delighting me with her fertile mind and showering me with her prayers, love, and encouragement.

An Umbrella
of Love

**You have been . . . a refuge for the needy in
his distress, a shelter from the storm.**
Isaiah 25:4

There is one gain that comes only to those who are
caught out in the rain, and it comes through God's dear
family. It is the blessing of finding oneself in the midst
of one of life's raging storms and yet be sheltered under
the faithful care of God's people—covered over by
intercessory prayer—protected by practical acts of love.
My family and I are standing, right now, beneath just
such an umbrella of love, and it is precious beyond
description.

I would not have signed up for this blessing, yet I
would not trade for anything on earth this sense of

being enfolded in God's vast family. All around the world people are praying for my husband, Herb, in his battle with cancer. Letters, cards, calls, and notes of encouragement have come daily with promises of prayer and reminders of God's faithfulness in spite of the steady progression of this terrible disease.

Sometimes I picture God being pelted with prayers and pleas on my husband's behalf.

Then my dear encourager, Mary Myers, wrote from Florida, painting a slightly different scene. She had been 'visiting us' via one of her creative prayer-times and wrote, "A little bit ago I dropped in your place with a few promises for Herb, and he was one sight to behold!"

And this is what she saw, in spite of the fact that she has been physically blinded by macular degeneration: "He was lying on, wrapped up in, festooned with, covered over with thousands and thousands of prayers and promises, promises and prayers; and the glory and fragrance filled your home and hearts."

And I breathed, recalling the "golden bowls full of incense, which are the prayers of the saints" (Revelation 5:8).

"So," Mary went on, "I left my greeting atop all the others—and the sight of Herb so festooned set me to quietly laughing inside, and I haven't quit yet."

And the picture of frail, white-haired Mary lying alone in bed (quite ill herself) laughing in the joy of the Lord and in the loving prayers of God's great family, set me to smiling and rejoicing inside. And I found that I, too, wanted to decorate others just as beautifully.

So I sent out prayers and promises, promises and prayers, to cover Mary and all of you, my dear brothers and sisters in Christ, who have prayed in loving faith seeking God's very best for us as we trust Him day by day.

And this is my prayer: that your love may abound more and more in knowledge and depth of insight, so that you may be able to discern what is best and may be pure and blameless until the day of Christ, filled with the fruit of righteousness that comes through Jesus Christ—to the glory and praise of God.

For this reason I kneel before the Father, from whom his whole family in heaven and earth derives its name. I pray that out of his glorious riches he may strengthen you with power through his Spirit in your inner being, so that Christ may dwell in your hearts through faith. And I pray that you, being rooted and established in love, may have power, together with all the saints, to grasp how wide and long and high and deep is the love of Christ, and to know this love that surpasses knowledge—that you may be filled to the measure of all the fullness of God.

—Ephesians 3:14–19

I'm Growing!

But grow in the grace and knowledge of our Lord and Savior, Jesus Christ. To him be glory both now and forever! Amen.
2 Peter 3:18

I keep reaching for You,
God,
and over and over I
find that
You reached first,
and so much
farther.
I keep reaching for You
Lord,
and over and over I

find that
I touch others
on my way to You.
I keep reaching for You,
Jesus,
and over and over I
find that
my arms are stretching.
I'm growing

I'm off and running, and I'm not turning back.

So let's keep focused on that goal, those of us who
want everything God has for us. If any of you have
something else in mind, something less than total
commitment, God will clear your blurred vision—
you'll see it yet! Now that we're on the right track,
let's stay on it.

Stick with me, friends. . . .

We're waiting the arrival of the Savior, the Master, Jesus Christ, who will transform our earthly
bodies into glorious bodies like his own. He'll make
us beautiful and whole with the same powerful skill

by which he is putting everything as it should be, under and around him.

My dear, dear friends! I love you so much. I do want the very best for you. You make me feel such joy, fill me with such pride. Don't waver. Stay on track, steady in God.

—*From Philippians 3:14–4:1, The Message*

Note to the Reader

The publisher invites you to share your response to the message of this book by writing Discovery House Publishers, P.O. Box 3566, Grand Rapids, MI 49501, U.S.A. or by calling 1-8 00-653-8333. For information about other Discovery House publications, contact us at the same address and phone number.